FIRE Starter

The Ultimate Guide to Achieving
Financial Independence and
Retiring Early

Chapter 1: Introduction

Welcome to the exciting world of FIRE! This book is the perfect introduction to the concept of Financial Independence, Retire Early, or FIRE, and it's packed with tips, tricks, and strategies to help you achieve your financial goals.

So, what is FIRE? FIRE is a movement that's all about achieving financial independence and retiring early. It's about taking control of your finances and your life, and living life on your own terms. FIRE is about having the freedom to do what you want, when you want, without having to worry about money.

Why is FIRE important? Well, for starters, it's a way to achieve financial freedom and retire early. By following the principles of FIRE, you can build a portfolio of assets that generate passive income and support your lifestyle without relying on traditional employment. This means you can retire early and spend your time doing the things you love, whether it's traveling, spending time with family and friends, or pursuing your passions.

But FIRE is about more than just retiring early. It's about taking control of your finances and your life. It's about being intentional with your money and your time, and living a life that's aligned with your values and priorities. FIRE is about achieving financial independence, but it's also about achieving personal freedom and fulfillment.

So, why should you read this book? Well, this book stands out because it's not just another dry, boring book about finance. This book is exciting, engaging, and packed with practical tips and strategies to help you achieve your financial goals. Whether you're just starting out on your FIRE journey or you're a seasoned pro, this book has something for everyone.

In this book, you'll learn how to assess your current financial situation, calculate your FIRE number, save money, invest for long-term growth, and more. You'll also get tips and tricks for making the most of your money and your time, and you'll be inspired to live a life that's aligned with your values and priorities.

So, if you're ready to take control of your finances and your life, and achieve financial independence and retire early, then this book is for you. Get ready to be inspired, motivated, and empowered to live the life of your dreams. Let's get started on your journey to FIRE!

Chapter 2: Assess Your Current Financial Situation

Before embarking on the journey to achieving FIRE, it is important to know where you stand financially. Assessing your current financial situation is the first step towards achieving financial independence and retiring early. In this chapter, we will discuss the importance of knowing where you stand financially and provide a simple exercise for readers to assess their current financial situation.

Why Knowing Your Current Financial Situation is Important

Assessing your current financial situation is important for several reasons. Firstly, it helps you understand your financial strengths and weaknesses. Knowing your financial strengths can help you capitalize on them to achieve your financial goals, while knowing your financial weaknesses can help you identify areas that require improvement.

Secondly, knowing your current financial situation helps you set realistic financial goals. By understanding your income, expenses, and debt, you can set achievable financial goals that align with your lifestyle and priorities.

Finally, assessing your current financial situation is critical for tracking your progress towards financial independence. By tracking your income, expenses, and debt over time, you can measure your progress towards your financial goals and make adjustments as needed.

Assessing Your Current Financial Situation: A Simple Exercise

To assess your current financial situation, start by gathering your financial statements and bills. This includes your bank statements, credit card statements, mortgage or rent statements, utility bills, and any other financial documents that pertain to your income and expenses.

Next, create a simple spreadsheet or use a financial tracking tool to record your income, expenses, and debt. This will help you see a clear picture of your current financial situation.

Start by recording your monthly income, including your salary, investment income, and any other sources of income. Next, record your monthly expenses, including fixed expenses like rent or mortgage payments, utilities, and car payments, as well as variable expenses like groceries, entertainment, and travel.

Finally, record your debt, including credit card debt, student loans, and any other outstanding loans. Be sure to record the interest rates and minimum payments for each debt.

Once you have recorded your income, expenses, and debt, take a close look at your financial situation. Are you spending more than you earn? Are you carrying a lot of debt? Are there areas where you can cut back on expenses?

Use this assessment to identify areas where you can improve your financial situation. This may include cutting back on expenses, increasing your income, or paying down debt. By taking the time to assess your current financial situation, you are setting yourself up for success on the path towards achieving financial independence and retiring early.

Chapter 3: Calculate Your FIRE Number

Now that you have assessed your current financial situation, it's time to calculate your FIRE number. Your FIRE number is the amount of money you need to accumulate to achieve financial independence and retire early. In this chapter, we will define what a FIRE number is, why it's important, and provide a simple formula for calculating your own FIRE number.

What is a FIRE Number and Why is it Important?

Your FIRE number is the amount of money you need to accumulate to support your lifestyle without relying on traditional employment. This includes all of your living expenses, such as housing, food, transportation, and entertainment, as well as any additional expenses you may have, such as travel or healthcare.

Knowing your FIRE number is important for several reasons. Firstly, it helps you set achievable financial goals. By knowing how much money you need to accumulate to achieve financial independence, you can set realistic financial goals that align with your lifestyle and priorities.

Secondly, knowing your FIRE number helps you track your progress towards financial independence. By monitoring your progress towards your FIRE number, you can make adjustments to your savings and investment strategy as needed.

Finally, knowing your FIRE number helps you make informed financial decisions. By understanding how much money you need to accumulate to achieve financial independence, you can make better decisions about your expenses, investments, and retirement plans.

Calculating Your FIRE Number: A Simple Formula

Calculating your FIRE number is easier than you might think. Here's a simple formula to help you calculate your FIRE number:

Annual Expenses x 25 = FIRE Number

To calculate your FIRE number, start by estimating your annual expenses. This includes all of your living expenses, such as housing, food, transportation, and entertainment, as well as any additional expenses you may have, such as travel or healthcare. Be sure to account for any expected changes in expenses, such as inflation or changes in your lifestyle.

Next, multiply your estimated annual expenses by 25. This is a common rule of thumb used in the FIRE community to estimate the amount of money you need to accumulate to achieve financial independence. The idea is that you can withdraw 4% of your portfolio each year in retirement without running out of money, so multiplying your annual expenses by 25 gives you a rough estimate of the amount of money you need to accumulate to support your lifestyle without relying on traditional employment.

For example, if your annual expenses are $50,000, your FIRE number would be $1,250,000 ($50,000 x 25).

Once you have calculated your FIRE number, you can start working towards achieving it by saving and investing strategically. While achieving financial independence and retiring early may seem daunting, calculating your FIRE number is a simple first step towards achieving your financial goals.

Chapter 4: The Power of Saving

Saving is a key component of achieving financial independence and retiring early. By saving money, you can reduce your reliance on traditional employment and accelerate your progress towards your financial goals. In this chapter, we will discuss the importance of saving for achieving FIRE and share tips and tricks for cutting expenses and increasing savings.

Why Saving is Important for Achieving FIRE

Saving is important for achieving FIRE for several reasons. Firstly, it helps you accumulate the wealth you need to support your lifestyle without relying on traditional employment. By saving a portion of your income each month, you can build a portfolio of investments that generate passive income and support your financial independence.

Secondly, saving helps you build a safety net for unexpected expenses. By having a savings cushion, you can weather unexpected expenses without derailing your progress towards financial independence.

Finally, saving is important for achieving financial freedom and retiring early. By reducing your expenses and increasing your savings, you can accelerate your progress towards your FIRE number and retire early.

Tips and Tricks for Cutting Expenses and Increasing Savings

There are many ways to cut expenses and increase savings. Here are a few tips and tricks to help you get started:

Create a Budget

Creating a budget is the first step towards cutting expenses and increasing savings. A budget helps you track your income and expenses and identify areas where you can reduce spending.

Cut Back on Non-Essential Expenses

Look for ways to cut back on non-essential expenses, such as dining out, entertainment, and travel. Consider packing your lunch for work, hosting a potluck instead of going out to eat, or taking a staycation instead of a costly vacation.

Reduce Your Housing Costs

Housing is often the largest expense for most people. Look for ways to reduce your housing costs, such as downsizing to a smaller home or apartment, getting a roommate, or moving to a more affordable area.

Increase Your Income

Look for ways to increase your income, such as negotiating a raise at work, taking on a side hustle, or investing in a passive income stream.

Automate Your Savings

Set up automatic transfers from your checking account to a savings account or investment account each month. This makes saving easier and ensures you are making progress towards your financial goals.

By cutting expenses and increasing savings, you can accelerate your progress towards financial independence and retiring early. While it may take some effort and sacrifice, the power of saving can help you achieve your financial goals and live life on your own terms.

Chapter 5: Investing for Long-Term Growth

Investing is a critical component of achieving financial independence and retiring early. By investing your money, you can achieve long-term growth and build a portfolio of assets that generate passive income. In this chapter, we will explain why investing is important for achieving FIRE and provide an overview of different investment vehicles and strategies for long-term growth.

Why Investing is Critical for Achieving FIRE

Investing is critical for achieving FIRE for several reasons. Firstly, it helps you grow your wealth over time. By investing your money in assets that appreciate in value, such as stocks and real estate, you can achieve long-term growth and build a portfolio of assets that generate passive income.

Secondly, investing helps you beat inflation. Inflation erodes the value of your money over time, which means you need to earn a return on your investments that exceeds the rate of inflation to maintain your purchasing power. Finally, investing helps you diversify your income streams. By investing in different assets and markets, you can reduce your reliance on traditional employment and generate passive income that supports your financial independence.

Investment Vehicles and Strategies for Long-Term Growth

There are many different investment vehicles and strategies for long-term growth. Here are a few examples:

Stocks

Investing in stocks is one of the most common strategies for achieving long-term growth. Stocks have historically provided high returns over the long term, although they can be volatile in the short term. Consider investing in a diversified portfolio of stocks through a low-cost index fund or exchange-traded fund (ETF).

Real Estate

Investing in real estate is another popular strategy for achieving long-term growth. Real estate has historically appreciated in value over time and can generate rental income. Consider investing in a rental property or a real estate investment trust (REIT).

Bonds

Investing in bonds is a lower-risk strategy for achieving long-term growth. Bonds provide a fixed income stream and are less volatile than stocks. Consider investing in a diversified portfolio of bonds through a bond fund or ETF.

Retirement Accounts

Investing in retirement accounts, such as a 401(k) or IRA, is a tax-efficient way to save for retirement. These accounts offer tax advantages that can help you save more money over the long term.

Diversification

Diversification is a key strategy for reducing risk and achieving long-term growth. By investing in different asset classes and markets, you can reduce your risk and improve your chances of achieving long-term growth.

Tips and Tricks for Making the Most of This Book

Here are a few tips and tricks for making the most of this book:

Take Action

Don't just read this book, take action. Use the tips and strategies provided to assess your current financial situation, calculate your FIRE number, and develop a plan for achieving your financial goals.

Stay Motivated

Achieving FIRE is a long-term goal that requires commitment and dedication. Stay motivated by setting short-term goals and celebrating your progress along the way.

Seek Help

Don't be afraid to seek help if you need it. Consider hiring a financial advisor or joining a FIRE community for support and guidance.

By investing for long-term growth and following the tips and strategies provided in this book, you can achieve financial independence and retire early.

Chapter 6: The Role of Passive Income in Achieving FIRE

Passive income is a key component of achieving financial independence and retiring early. By generating passive income streams, you can reduce your reliance on traditional employment and build a portfolio of assets that generate income even when you're not working. In this chapter, we will define what passive income is, why it's important for achieving FIRE, and provide examples of different types of passive income streams.

What is Passive Income and Why is it Important for Achieving FIRE?

Passive income is income that you earn without having to actively work for it. This can include rental income, dividend income, interest income, and capital gains. Passive income is important for achieving FIRE because it allows you to generate income even when you're not working, which means you can support your lifestyle without relying on traditional employment. Passive income is also important because it can provide a source of income that's not subject to the volatility of the stock market or the economy. By building a diversified portfolio of passive income streams, you can reduce your risk and improve your chances of achieving financial independence and retiring early.

Examples of Different Types of Passive Income Streams

There are many different types of passive income streams. Here are a few examples:

Rental Income

Rental income is a common type of passive income stream. By owning rental properties, you can generate rental income that covers your expenses and provides a source of passive income.

Dividend Income

Dividend income is income that you earn from owning stocks that pay dividends. Dividend-paying stocks are a popular choice for generating passive income because they provide a regular income stream without requiring you to sell your assets.

Interest Income

Interest income is income that you earn from owning bonds, CDs, or other fixed-income investments. While interest rates are currently low, interest income can still provide a source of passive income.

Royalty Income

Royalty income is income that you earn from licensing your intellectual property, such as books, music, or patents. While not everyone has intellectual property to license, it's a potential source of passive income for those who do.

Capital Gains

Capital gains are the profits you earn from selling an asset that has appreciated in value. While not technically passive income, capital gains can be a source of income if you sell your assets strategically and reinvest the profits in passive income streams.

By building a diversified portfolio of passive income streams, you can reduce your reliance on traditional employment and accelerate your progress towards financial independence and retiring early. While building passive income streams may take time and effort, the benefits of achieving financial freedom and living life on your own terms make it well worth the effort.

Chapter 7: The Mindset Shift Needed for FIRE Success

Achieving financial independence and retiring early requires more than just financial know-how. It requires a mindset shift towards financial freedom and a willingness to make sacrifices and take risks to achieve your goals. In this chapter, we will discuss the importance of mindset and how it can impact your ability to achieve FIRE. We'll also share tips and tricks for shifting your mindset towards financial freedom.

The Importance of Mindset for Achieving FIRE

Your mindset can have a significant impact on your ability to achieve FIRE. If you have a scarcity mindset, for example, you may struggle to save money and make the necessary sacrifices to achieve your financial goals. On the other hand, if you have an abundance mindset, you may be more willing to take risks and make the necessary sacrifices to achieve financial freedom. In addition, your mindset can impact your relationship with money. If you have a negative mindset towards money, you may struggle to manage your finances effectively and make wise financial decisions. By shifting your mindset towards financial freedom, you can improve your relationship with money and achieve your financial goals more effectively.

Tips and Tricks for Shifting Your Mindset towards Financial Freedom

Here are a few tips and tricks for shifting your mindset towards financial freedom:

Define Your Why

Before you can shift your mindset towards financial freedom, it's important to define your why. Why do you want to achieve financial independence? What's driving you to pursue this goal? By defining your why, you can stay motivated and focused on your financial goals.

Practice Gratitude

Practicing gratitude is a powerful way to shift your mindset towards financial freedom. By focusing on what you already have and being grateful for it, you can reduce your focus on material possessions and improve your relationship with money.

Embrace Frugality

Embracing frugality is another powerful way to shift your mindset towards financial freedom. By living below your means and being intentional with your spending, you can reduce your reliance on traditional employment and accelerate your progress towards financial independence.

Take Calculated Risks

Taking calculated risks is a key component of achieving financial independence and retiring early. By being willing to take risks and invest in your future, you can accelerate your progress towards your financial goals and achieve financial freedom more quickly.

Seek Inspiration

Finally, seek inspiration from others who have achieved financial independence and retired early. Join a FIRE community, read blogs and books on the subject, and surround yourself with like-minded individuals who can offer support and guidance on your journey.

By shifting your mindset towards financial freedom and following the tips and tricks provided in this chapter, you can improve your relationship with money, accelerate your progress towards financial independence, and achieve your goal of retiring early.

Chapter 8: Dealing with Debt

Debt can be a major obstacle to achieving financial independence and retiring early. High levels of debt can limit your ability to save money, invest for the future, and achieve your financial goals. In this chapter, we will discuss the impact of debt on achieving FIRE and provide strategies for paying off debt and avoiding debt in the future.

The Impact of Debt on Achieving FIRE

Debt can have a significant impact on your ability to achieve financial independence and retire early. High levels of debt can limit your ability to save money and invest for the future, which means it can take longer to achieve your financial goals. Debt can also increase your financial risk, making it more difficult to achieve financial stability and security.

In addition, debt can impact your mental and emotional well-being. If you're struggling with debt, it can cause stress, anxiety, and worry, which can negatively impact your overall quality of life.

Strategies for Paying Off Debt and Avoiding Debt in the Future

Here are a few strategies for paying off debt and avoiding debt in the future:

Make a Plan

The first step in paying off debt is to make a plan. Take stock of your debt and create a plan for paying it off, prioritizing the debt with the highest interest rates first. Consider using a debt repayment calculator to help you create a plan that's realistic and achievable.

Cut Expenses

Cutting expenses is a key component of paying off debt. Look for ways to reduce your expenses and redirect that money towards paying off your debt. Consider cutting back on discretionary expenses, such as eating out or shopping, and redirecting that money towards your debt.

Increase Income

Increasing your income is another way to pay off debt more quickly. Consider taking on a side hustle or freelance work to increase your income and put more money towards paying off your debt.

Avoid Taking on More Debt

Avoiding taking on more debt is key to achieving financial independence and retiring early. Look for ways to avoid taking on new debt, such as paying cash for purchases and avoiding high-interest loans and credit cards.

Seek Help

If you're struggling with debt, don't be afraid to seek help. Consider reaching out to a financial advisor or credit counselor for guidance and support.

By paying off debt and avoiding debt in the future, you can reduce your financial risk and accelerate your progress towards financial independence and retiring early. While it may take time and effort to pay off debt, the benefits of achieving financial freedom and living life on your own terms make it well worth the effort.

Chapter 9: Building Your Emergency Fund

An emergency fund is a critical component of achieving financial independence and retiring early. An emergency fund is a sum of money that you set aside to cover unexpected expenses, such as medical bills or car repairs. In this chapter, we will discuss the importance of having an emergency fund and share tips for building and maintaining an emergency fund.

The Importance of Having an Emergency Fund

Having an emergency fund is important for several reasons. First, it can provide peace of mind, knowing that you have a cushion to fall back on in case of an unexpected expense. Second, an emergency fund can help you avoid taking on debt or using high-interest credit cards to cover unexpected expenses. Third, an emergency fund can help you stay on track towards your financial goals by avoiding setbacks that can derail your progress.

Tips for Building and Maintaining an Emergency Fund

Here are a few tips for building and maintaining an emergency fund:

Set a Goal

The first step in building an emergency fund is to set a goal. Aim to save at least three to six months' worth of living expenses in your emergency fund. This can help you cover unexpected expenses without derailing your progress towards financial independence and retiring early.

Automate Your Savings

Automating your savings is a powerful way to build your emergency fund. Set up automatic transfers from your checking account to your emergency fund each month to ensure that you're consistently saving towards your goal.

Cut Expenses

Cutting expenses is another way to build your emergency fund more quickly. Look for ways to reduce your expenses and redirect that money towards your emergency fund. Consider cutting back on discretionary expenses, such as eating out or shopping, and redirecting that money towards your emergency fund.

Keep Your Emergency Fund Separate

Keep your emergency fund separate from your other accounts to avoid the temptation to use it for non-emergency expenses. Consider opening a separate savings account specifically for your emergency fund.

Replenish Your Fund

Finally, it's important to replenish your emergency fund after using it for an unexpected expense. Make a plan to replenish your emergency fund as quickly as possible to ensure that you're always prepared for the unexpected.

By building and maintaining an emergency fund, you can reduce your financial risk and improve your chances of achieving financial independence and retiring early. While building an emergency fund may take time and effort, the peace of mind that comes with knowing you're prepared for the unexpected is well worth the effort.

Chapter 10: Making Your Money Work for You

To achieve financial independence and retire early, it's important to make your money work for you. This means optimizing your finances to maximize returns and minimize expenses. In this chapter, we will discuss the importance of optimizing your finances and share tips for finding the best financial products and services for your needs.

The Importance of Optimizing Your Finances

Optimizing your finances is important for several reasons. First, it can help you maximize your returns and achieve your financial goals more quickly. Second, it can help you minimize expenses and reduce your reliance on traditional employment. Third, it can help you manage risk and protect your assets from market volatility.

Tips for Finding the Best Financial Products and Services for Your Needs

Here are a few tips for finding the best financial products and services for your needs:

Research Your Options

The first step in finding the best financial products and services for your needs is to do your research. Look for financial products and services that offer the best returns and lowest fees. Consider using online tools and resources to compare different options and find the best deals.

Consider Your Risk Tolerance

When choosing financial products and services, it's important to consider your risk tolerance. If you're risk-averse, you may want to focus on conservative investments that offer low-risk, low-return options. If you're willing to take on more risk, you may want to consider more aggressive investments that offer higher returns but also higher risk.

Diversify Your Investments

Diversifying your investments is a key component of optimizing your finances. By spreading your investments across different asset classes and products, you can reduce your risk and improve your chances of achieving your financial goals.

Seek Professional Advice

If you're unsure about which financial products and services to choose, consider seeking professional advice. A financial advisor can help you navigate the complexities of the financial world and make informed decisions about your investments.

Stay Up to Date

Finally, it's important to stay up to date on the latest financial products and services. The financial world is constantly evolving, and staying informed can help you make the best decisions for your financial future.

By optimizing your finances and finding the best financial products and services for your needs, you can maximize your returns, minimize expenses, and achieve your financial goals more quickly. While it may take time and effort to find the best options, the benefits of achieving financial independence and retiring early make it well worth the effort.

Chapter 11: The Importance of Education and Continued Learning

Achieving financial independence and retiring early requires more than just financial know-how. It requires a commitment to ongoing education and continued learning to stay up-to-date on best practices and improve your financial literacy. In this chapter, we will discuss the importance of education and continued learning for achieving FIRE and share tips and resources for improving financial literacy and staying up-to-date on best practices.

The Importance of Education and Continued Learning for Achieving FIRE

Education and continued learning are important for several reasons. First, it can help you stay informed about new investment opportunities and financial products that can help you achieve your financial goals more quickly. Second, it can help you avoid costly mistakes and reduce your financial risk. Third, it can help you develop the skills and knowledge you need to manage your finances effectively and make informed financial decisions.

Tips and Resources for Improving Financial Literacy and Staying Up-to-Date on Best Practices

Here are a few tips and resources for improving financial literacy and staying up-to-date on best practices:

Read Books and Blogs

Reading books and blogs on personal finance is a great way to improve your financial literacy and stay informed about new investment opportunities and financial products. Look for books and blogs written by reputable authors and financial experts to ensure that you're getting reliable information.

Take Online Courses

Taking online courses on personal finance and investing is another way to improve your financial literacy and stay up-to-date on best practices. Consider taking courses from reputable institutions or online platforms to ensure that you're getting high-quality education.

Attend Seminars and Workshops

Attending seminars and workshops on personal finance and investing is a great way to learn from experts and network with like-minded individuals. Look for seminars and workshops in your area or attend online events to learn from experts and gain valuable insights.

Join a Community

Joining a community of like-minded individuals is a powerful way to stay motivated and learn from others. Look for online communities or local groups that focus on personal finance and investing to connect with others and share knowledge and resources.

Work with a Financial Advisor

Finally, consider working with a financial advisor to improve your financial literacy and get personalized advice and guidance. A financial advisor can help you develop a comprehensive financial plan and provide ongoing support and education to help you achieve your financial goals.

By committing to ongoing education and continued learning, you can improve your financial literacy, stay up-to-date on best practices, and achieve financial independence and retire early more quickly and effectively. While it may take time and effort to stay informed and educated, the benefits of achieving financial freedom and living life on your own terms make it well worth the effort.

Chapter 12: Staying the Course

Achieving financial independence and retiring early is a long-term journey that requires commitment, focus, and dedication. While it may be challenging at times, staying the course and remaining committed to your goals is essential for success. In this chapter, we will discuss the importance of staying committed to the FIRE journey and share tips and tricks for staying motivated and focused on your goals.

The Importance of Staying Committed to the FIRE Journey

Staying committed to the FIRE journey is important for several reasons. First, it can help you stay motivated and focused on your goals, even when faced with challenges or setbacks. Second, it can help you develop the discipline and resilience you need to succeed in the long-term. Third, it can help you stay on track towards achieving financial independence and retiring early, even when life gets in the way.

Tips and Tricks for Staying Motivated and Focused on Your Goals

Here are a few tips and tricks for staying motivated and focused on your goals:

Set Realistic Goals

Setting realistic goals is an important part of staying committed to the FIRE journey. Be sure to set goals that are achievable and realistic based on your current financial situation and lifestyle.

Track Your Progress

Tracking your progress is a powerful way to stay motivated and focused on your goals. Use tools like spreadsheets, financial apps, or journals to track your progress towards achieving your financial goals.

Celebrate Your Wins

Celebrating your wins along the way is important for staying motivated and focused on your goals. Take time to acknowledge and celebrate your progress, no matter how small.

Find Support

Finding support from family, friends, or a community of like-minded individuals can help you stay motivated and focused on your goals. Look for online communities or local groups that focus on personal finance and investing to connect with others and share knowledge and resources.

Stay Positive

Finally, it's important to stay positive and maintain a growth mindset throughout the FIRE journey. Embrace challenges and setbacks as opportunities to learn and grow, and focus on the progress you've made towards achieving your financial goals.

By staying committed to the FIRE journey and using these tips and tricks to stay motivated and focused on your goals, you can achieve financial independence and retire early more quickly and effectively. While it may take time and effort to stay the course, the benefits of achieving financial freedom and living life on your own terms make it well worth the effort.

Chapter 13: Retiring Early: What to Expect

Retiring early is the ultimate goal of the FIRE journey, but what does it really entail? In this chapter, we will discuss what readers can expect when they achieve FIRE and retire early, as well as provide tips for adjusting to early retirement and maximizing your retirement lifestyle.

What to Expect When You Achieve FIRE and Retire Early

Achieving financial independence and retiring early means having the financial freedom to live life on your own terms. It means having the ability to retire from traditional employment, pursue your passions and interests, travel, or spend time with family and friends. However, retiring early also comes with its own set of challenges and considerations.

For example, retiring early may mean having to adjust to a new lifestyle and finding meaningful ways to spend your time. It may also mean managing your finances differently, as you no longer have a regular paycheck to rely on. Additionally, retiring early may mean having to navigate healthcare and other expenses without the support of an employer-sponsored plan.

Tips for Adjusting to Early Retirement and Maximizing Your Retirement Lifestyle

Here are a few tips for adjusting to early retirement and maximizing your retirement lifestyle:

Plan Ahead

Planning ahead is critical for adjusting to early retirement and ensuring that you have the resources you need to support your lifestyle. Be sure to create a comprehensive retirement plan that takes into account your lifestyle goals and financial needs.

Stay Active

Staying active and engaged in your community and hobbies is important for maintaining your mental and physical health during retirement. Look for opportunities to volunteer, join clubs or groups, or pursue new interests to stay engaged and active.

Manage Your Finances

Managing your finances effectively is critical for making your retirement lifestyle sustainable. Be sure to create a budget, monitor your expenses, and explore strategies for generating passive income to supplement your retirement savings.

Stay Connected

Staying connected with family and friends is important for maintaining your social connections and support system during retirement. Make an effort to stay in touch with loved ones and seek out opportunities to connect with new people.

Embrace Change

Finally, it's important to embrace change and be open to new experiences and opportunities during retirement. Embrace the freedom and flexibility that comes with early retirement and explore new ways to live your best life.

By following these tips and embracing the opportunities that come with early retirement, you can maximize your retirement lifestyle and enjoy the benefits of achieving financial independence and retiring early. While adjusting to early retirement may take time and effort, the rewards of living life on your own terms are well worth the journey.

Chapter 14: Achieving FIRE as a Family

Achieving financial independence and retiring early can be a team effort, and involving your family in your FIRE journey can have many benefits. In this chapter, we will discuss how to achieve FIRE as a family, the benefits of working towards financial independence together, and provide tips for involving your partner and children in your FIRE journey.

How to Achieve FIRE as a Family

Achieving FIRE as a family means setting shared goals and working together to achieve them. It means involving your partner and children in your financial planning, budgeting, and investing strategies. By involving your family in your FIRE journey, you can teach them valuable financial skills, build a stronger sense of teamwork, and create shared goals and aspirations.

Benefits of Working Towards Financial Independence Together

Working towards financial independence together as a family has many benefits. It can help you build stronger relationships, develop better communication skills, and teach your children valuable financial skills that they can use throughout their lives. Additionally, achieving FIRE as a family means having the financial freedom to spend more time together, travel, or pursue shared interests and passions.

Tips for Involving Your Partner and Children in Your FIRE Journey

Here are a few tips for involving your partner and children in your FIRE journey:

Set Shared Goals

Setting shared goals is critical for achieving FIRE as a family. Involve your partner and children in the goal-setting process and make sure that everyone is on the same page.

Communicate Openly

Communication is key for achieving FIRE as a family. Make sure that you and your partner are communicating openly and honestly about your financial goals and strategies. Additionally, involve your children in conversations about money and finances to help them develop good financial habits.

Create a Budget

Creating a budget is an important part of achieving FIRE as a family. Involve your partner and children in the budgeting process and make sure that everyone is aware of your family's income, expenses, and financial goals.

Teach Financial Skills

Teaching your children financial skills is an important part of achieving FIRE as a family. Look for opportunities to teach your children about budgeting, saving, and investing, and involve them in your family's financial decisions.

Celebrate Together

Celebrating your successes as a family is important for building a sense of teamwork and motivation. Make sure that you celebrate your financial wins together and take time to acknowledge and appreciate the hard work that you've put in to achieve your goals.

By involving your partner and children in your FIRE journey and using these tips to work towards financial independence as a family, you can build stronger relationships, develop better communication skills, and achieve your financial goals more quickly and effectively. While it may take time and effort to involve your family in your FIRE journey, the rewards of achieving financial independence as a team are well worth the effort.

Chapter 15: The Role of Side Hustles in Achieving FIRE

A side hustle is a way to earn extra income outside of your regular job or business. While it may seem like a daunting task to take on additional work, side hustles can play a significant role in achieving financial independence and retiring early. In this chapter, we will define what a side hustle is, discuss how it can help you achieve FIRE faster, and provide examples of profitable side hustles and tips for starting your own.

What is a Side Hustle and How Can It Help You Achieve FIRE Faster?

A side hustle is a flexible way to earn extra income that can help you achieve financial independence and retire early faster. By earning extra income, you can accelerate your savings and investment goals, pay off debt faster, and build a larger nest egg for retirement. Additionally, side hustles can help you diversify your income streams and reduce your reliance on a single source of income.

Examples of Profitable Side Hustles and Tips for Starting Your Own

Here are a few examples of profitable side hustles and tips for starting your own:

Freelance Work

Freelance work is a flexible and profitable side hustle that can be done from anywhere. Consider offering your skills as a writer, designer, or programmer on websites like Upwork, Freelancer, or Fiverr.

Online Selling

Online selling is another profitable side hustle that can be done from home. Consider selling items on platforms like Amazon, eBay, or Etsy, or starting your own online store.

Renting Property

Renting property is a lucrative side hustle that can generate passive income. Consider renting out a spare room on Airbnb or renting out property on websites like Vrbo or HomeAway.

Pet Sitting or Dog Walking

Pet sitting or dog walking is a fun and flexible side hustle that can be done in your spare time. Consider offering your services on websites like Rover or Wag.

Consulting

Consulting is a profitable side hustle that allows you to use your expertise to help others. Consider offering your services as a consultant in your field of expertise on websites like Clarity or Highbrow.

When starting your own side hustle, it's important to consider your skills, interests, and availability. Look for opportunities to monetize your hobbies or interests, and make sure that you're offering something of value to your customers. Additionally, be sure to create a plan for managing your time and resources effectively to ensure that your side hustle doesn't interfere with your regular job or business.

By starting a side hustle and using it to generate extra income, you can accelerate your journey towards financial independence and retiring early. While it may require some effort and time management, the benefits of diversifying your income streams and achieving your financial goals faster are well worth the effort.

Chapter 16: FIRE and Taxes

When pursuing financial independence and retiring early, taxes can have a significant impact on your ability to achieve your goals. In this chapter, we will discuss the impact of taxes on achieving FIRE, strategies for minimizing your tax liability, and provide tips for optimizing your tax situation for maximum savings.

The Impact of Taxes on Achieving FIRE

Taxes can have a significant impact on your ability to achieve FIRE. High tax rates, penalties for early withdrawals from retirement accounts, and the tax implications of generating passive income can all eat into your savings and slow down your progress towards financial independence. Additionally, taxes can be complex and confusing, making it difficult to navigate the tax code and take advantage of available deductions and credits.

Strategies for Minimizing Your Tax Liability

Here are a few strategies for minimizing your tax liability and optimizing your finances for maximum savings:

Maximize Your Retirement Contributions

One of the best ways to minimize your tax liability and build your retirement savings is to maximize your contributions to tax-advantaged retirement accounts like 401(k)s, IRAs, and HSAs. By doing so, you can reduce your taxable income and take advantage of tax-deferred growth.

Take Advantage of Tax Deductions and Credits

There are many tax deductions and credits available to help reduce your tax liability. Look for opportunities to take advantage of deductions and credits related to charitable donations, education expenses, and home ownership, among others.

Invest in Tax-Efficient Investments

Investing in tax-efficient investments like index funds and ETFs can help you minimize your tax liability and maximize your returns. These investments tend to have low turnover rates and generate minimal taxable income, making them an attractive option for long-term investors.

Consider Tax-Loss Harvesting

Tax-loss harvesting involves selling investments that have lost value in order to offset capital gains and reduce your tax liability. This strategy can be a valuable tool for minimizing your tax liability and optimizing your investment portfolio.

Optimizing Your Tax Situation for Maximum Savings

To optimize your tax situation for maximum savings, it's important to stay informed about changes to the tax code and seek out opportunities to reduce your tax liability. Additionally, consider working with a tax professional to help you navigate the complexities of the tax code and identify opportunities for savings.

By implementing these strategies and staying informed about changes to the tax code, you can minimize your tax liability and optimize your finances for maximum savings. While navigating the tax code may seem daunting, the benefits of minimizing your tax liability and accelerating your journey towards financial independence and retiring early are well worth the effort.

Chapter 17: Achieving FIRE on a Tight Budget

Achieving financial independence and retiring early may seem daunting if you have limited resources, but it is possible. In this chapter, we will discuss how to achieve FIRE on a tight budget, and provide tips and strategies for maximizing your savings and investments.

How to Achieve FIRE on a Tight Budget

Achieving FIRE on a tight budget requires a commitment to saving and investing, as well as a willingness to make sacrifices and live within your means. It requires a focus on the long-term and a willingness to delay gratification in order to achieve your financial goals. Here are a few tips for achieving FIRE on a tight budget:

Set Realistic Goals

When pursuing FIRE on a tight budget, it's important to set realistic goals that align with your financial situation. This may mean setting a lower FIRE number or a longer timeline for achieving financial independence.

Cut Expenses

Cutting expenses is critical for achieving FIRE on a tight budget. Look for opportunities to reduce your monthly expenses, such as cutting back on dining out, reducing your utility bills, or downsizing your home.

Increase Your Income

Increasing your income is another way to achieve FIRE on a tight budget. Consider taking on a side hustle, freelancing, or starting a small business to generate extra income.

Focus on High-Yield Investments

When investing on a tight budget, it's important to focus on high-yield investments that offer the potential for maximum returns. Look for low-cost, diversified index funds or ETFs that offer long-term growth potential.

Tips and Strategies for Maximizing Your Savings and Investments on a Tight Budget

Here are a few tips and strategies for maximizing your savings and investments on a tight budget:

Automate Your Savings

Automating your savings is an effective way to build your savings and investments over time. Consider setting up automatic transfers from your checking account to a savings or investment account each month.

Maximize Tax-Advantaged Accounts

Maximize your contributions to tax-advantaged retirement accounts, such as 401(k)s, IRAs, or HSAs, to minimize your tax liability and accelerate your savings.

Use Debt Wisely

If you have debt, focus on paying off high-interest debt first, and avoid taking on new debt unless it is necessary. Consider using debt consolidation or refinancing strategies to reduce your interest rates and accelerate your debt payoff.

Stay Focused on Your Goals

Staying focused on your financial goals and remaining committed to your FIRE journey is critical when working with a tight budget. Celebrate your financial wins along the way and stay motivated by tracking your progress towards financial independence.

By implementing these tips and strategies, you can achieve financial independence and retire early on a tight budget. While it may require some sacrifices and hard work, the rewards of achieving FIRE and living a financially free life are well worth the effort.

Chapter 18: Achieving FIRE Later in Life

While achieving financial independence and retiring early may seem like a young person's game, it is possible to achieve FIRE later in life. In this chapter, we will discuss how to achieve FIRE even if you are starting later in life, and provide tips and strategies for catching up on retirement savings and building passive income streams.

How to Achieve FIRE Later in Life

Achieving FIRE later in life requires a commitment to saving and investing, as well as a willingness to make adjustments to your lifestyle and career. It requires a focus on the long-term and a willingness to delay gratification in order to achieve your financial goals. Here are a few tips for achieving FIRE later in life:

Assess Your Current Situation

When starting later in life, it's important to assess your current financial situation and determine how much you will need to save in order to achieve financial independence. Consider meeting with a financial advisor to help you determine your FIRE number.

Increase Your Income

Increasing your income is a critical component of achieving FIRE later in life. Consider taking on a second job, consulting, or starting a small business to generate extra income.

Cut Expenses

Cutting expenses is also critical for achieving FIRE later in life. Look for opportunities to reduce your monthly expenses, such as downsizing your home or cutting back on non-essential spending.

Focus on High-Yield Investments

When investing later in life, it's important to focus on high-yield investments that offer the potential for maximum returns. Look for low-cost, diversified index funds or ETFs that offer long-term growth potential.

Tips and Strategies for Catching Up on Retirement Savings and Building Passive Income Streams

Here are a few tips and strategies for catching up on retirement savings and building passive income streams:

Maximize Your Retirement Contributions

Maximize your contributions to tax-advantaged retirement accounts, such as 401(k)s, IRAs, or HSAs, to accelerate your retirement savings and minimize your tax liability.

Consider Real Estate Investing

Real estate investing can be a profitable way to build passive income streams and accelerate your journey towards financial independence. Consider investing in rental properties or real estate investment trusts (REITs).

Build a Portfolio of Dividend Stocks

Dividend stocks can be an attractive option for building passive income streams later in life. Look for stocks that pay regular dividends and have a history of increasing their payouts over time.

Stay Focused on Your Goals

Staying focused on your financial goals and remaining committed to your FIRE journey is critical when starting later in life. Celebrate your financial wins along the way and stay motivated by tracking your progress towards financial independence.

By implementing these tips and strategies, you can achieve financial independence and retire early later in life. While it may require some sacrifices and hard work, the rewards of achieving FIRE and living a financially free life are well worth the effort.

Chapter 19: Conclusion

Congratulations, you've made it to the end of the book! By now, you should have a solid understanding of what it takes to achieve FIRE (Financial Independence, Retire Early), and be equipped with the tools and strategies to help you get there. Let's take a moment to summarize the key takeaways from the book and encourage you to continue your journey towards financial freedom.

Key Takeaways

Financial Independence is Achievable: Achieving financial independence and retiring early is possible for anyone, regardless of your income or current financial situation. It requires commitment, hard work, and a willingness to make sacrifices along the way.

Saving and Investing are Key

Saving and investing are critical components of achieving FIRE. By living below your means and investing for the long-term, you can build the wealth necessary to achieve financial independence.

Passive Income is Powerful

Building passive income streams, such as rental properties, dividend stocks, or a successful side hustle, can help you achieve financial independence faster and provide a steady source of income in retirement.

Mindset Matters

Shifting your mindset towards financial freedom and adopting a long-term perspective is critical for achieving FIRE. Stay focused on your goals, celebrate your wins along the way, and don't let setbacks discourage you.

Continuing Your Journey

While this book provides a solid foundation for achieving FIRE, the journey towards financial independence is ongoing. It requires ongoing education, self-reflection, and a commitment to continuous improvement. Here are a few ways to continue your journey towards FIRE:

Stay Informed

Stay informed about changes to the tax code, investing strategies, and other financial news that may impact your journey towards financial independence.

Connect with Others

Connect with others in the FIRE community for support, encouragement, and accountability. Attend meetups, join online forums, and read blogs and books to stay connected.

Keep Learning

Continue to educate yourself about personal finance, investing, and entrepreneurship. Attend conferences, read books and blogs, and take courses to stay up-to-date on best practices.

Stay Committed

Stay committed to your goals and don't let setbacks discourage you. Remember that achieving FIRE is a long-term journey, and each small step you take along the way brings you closer to financial independence.

In conclusion, achieving FIRE is possible for anyone willing to put in the work and make the necessary sacrifices. By saving and investing for the long-term, building passive income streams, and adopting a mindset of financial freedom, you can achieve the financial independence necessary to retire early and live the life you've always dreamed of. Best of luck on your journey towards FIRE!